Joseph A. [signature]

VALLEY OF THE PINES
MONTAGUE, MICH.

VARIOUS VIEWS

VARIOUS VIEWS

BY

WILLIAM MORTON PAYNE

CHICAGO
A. C. McCLURG & CO.
1902

Copyright
A. C. McClurg & Co.
1902

Published October, 1902

Composition by The Dial Press, Chicago, U.S.A.
Presswork by The University Press, Cambridge, U.S.A.

TO
PAUL SHOREY
WITH
THIRTY YEARS OF FRIENDSHIP

PREFACE.

THIS book is a companion volume to 'Little Leaders' and 'Editorial Echoes.' Like its predecessors, it is made up of thirty leading articles written for 'The Dial' during recent years. A few inconsiderable changes in the original text have been made, but the papers remain substantially what they were when first printed, and even the conventional editorial style has been retained. The miscellaneous character of the papers here brought together has made impossible the threefold classification of the earlier volumes, although a rough grouping according to subject-matter has been attempted. It will be found, however, that, as before, the writer has been chiefly preoccupied with themes suggested by the broader aspects of literary history and criticism.

CHICAGO, October 1, 1902.

CONTENTS.

	PAGE
THE HUGO CENTENARY	11
ALEXANDER THE GREAT	22
SHAKESPEARE IN FRANCE	32
THE TIE THAT BINDS	42
INTERNATIONAL AMITY	50
HERO-WORSHIP	57
A PHILISTINE WATCHWORD	67
A QUESTION OF LITERARY CONSCIENCE	75
THE ARTIST AND THE MAN	83
THE DUTIES OF AUTHORS	93
TENDENCIES IN LITERATURE	102
ENERGY AND ART	109
THE ARCHITECTURE OF THE MIND	119
IDIOM AND IDEAL	128
THE REVALUATION OF LITERATURE	136
THE GENTLE READER	145
THE TRIUMPH OF THE NOVELIST	153
THE REVIVAL OF ROMANCE	161
THE GREAT AMERICAN NOVEL	169
THE NOVEL AND THE LIBRARY	178
THE DRAMA AS ART	189
THE ENDOWED THEATRE	198

CONTENTS — Continued.

	PAGE
M. Brunetière's Pedagogical Prescription	207
The Critic as Picker and Stealer	215
A Word for Minor Poetry	223
Newspaper Science	231
The Decay of American Journalism	242
The Star System in Publishing	251
The Young Person	260
The New Patriotic Impulse	269

THE HUGO CENTENARY.

SEVENTEEN years ago, the death of Victor Hugo, at the age of eighty-three, plunged into mourning the whole civilized world. At Goethe's age, and Voltaire's, within a few months, he entered into rest, and of all the great men of European letters since Shakespeare, those two alone seemed worthy to be named with him. For more than half a century, his rank had been preëminent, not among French writers alone, but among those of the whole world, and his venerable declining years had been crowned with such glory as is won by few indeed among the sons of men. His genius had so dominated the century which it illustrated that it seemed as if history must henceforth remember the period by his name, and speak of the Age of Hugo as it speaks of the Age of Dante or the Age of Shakespeare.

Now that the years of Victor Hugo's life, added to the years that have elapsed since his death, have made up the full sum of one hundred, and men touched with his spirit and inspired by his message are engaged — not alone in the country that has the first claim upon his memory — in recalling his splendid services to humanity and his priceless contributions to the treasury of that literature which has the breath of life everlasting, — now that the centennial year of his birth has been reached, it becomes pertinent to ask how time has dealt with his reputation, and how strong is still the hold of his works upon the artistic sense and the conscience of the generation that has come after him. The final appraisal is not yet possible, nor will it be for perhaps a hundred years to come, but some things may now be said that our posterity will not be likely to repudiate. For it must be remembered that Hugo's work has been tested by the apparatus of the critic during a much longer period than the term of years that he has been in his grave. It is now three-quarters of a century since the famous pronunciamento of 'Cromwell' was delivered, and it is nearly as long since the pitched battle between the romanticists and classicists that was occasioned by the *première* of 'Hernani.' During all that time, the genius of

Hugo has been hotly championed by some, and bitterly assailed by others. When he died, detraction had already done its worst upon him, and his fame had emerged well-nigh untarnished from the smoke of the critical conflict. Since 1885, his assailants have found nothing to say of him so severe as what was said long before that date, and the recognition of his finer qualities — always admitted by those who dealt with him the most roughly — has been less grudgingly admitted even by those who have felt bound to enter their caveat against his acceptance as one of the great figures in the history of literature.

We have observed with close attention the currents and counter-currents of recent opinion concerning Hugo's work, and it seems to us that there has gradually shaped itself, in the consciousness of his own compatriots as well as in the consciousness of the cosmopolitan tribunal of letters, an image of the poet that looms larger and larger as the age recedes from him, an image so colossal that it dwarfs all others of his world-contemporaries in the retrospective vision. Can we as Englishmen, great as must be our reverence for the memories of Shelley and Wordsworth and Tennyson, of Carlyle and Ruskin and Emerson, can we in fairness claim that any of these men matches Hugo in artistic and moral stature? Can a German make the claim for Heine, can an Italian make it for Signor Carducci, can a Russian make it for Tourguénieff, can a Norwegian make it for Dr. Ibsen? Can a Frenchman fairly make it for Musset or Balzac or Renan? To ask these questions, it seems to us, is to make it clear that negative answers are the only possible ones. Certain aspects of the genius of these other men may appeal to us more deeply, or strike more responsive chords in our consciousness, but the noblest personality of them all, with the sum total of its achievement, set beside the personality and the achievement of Hugo, must suffer in the comparison. 'The spiritual sovereign of the nineteenth century,' Mr. Swinburne calls him, and, whatever critical reservations we may make upon this point or upon that, it seems that the ascription is still the just due of the great poet, novelist, and dramatist whose writings have now been steadily pouring from the press for a period of nearly eighty years.

Against this secular canonization of the poet

the devil's advocate has advanced three main charges. The first is that, while parading omniscience, he is guilty of gross inaccuracies of scholarship and grotesque perversions of the truth. This charge may fairly be allowed. 'L'Homme Qui Rit,' for example, is a romance *pour rire* as far as its background of historical fact is concerned. 'Notre Dame de Paris,' with its 'deux tours de granit faites par Charlemagne,' is not in much better case, although its subject is the history of the poet's own country. In short, the story of Hugo's blunders is as lengthy as it is amusing. The second charge is that he is a rhetorician, who cultivated a turgid, bombastic, and sensational manner of composition, instead of following in the footsteps of the great masters of style. This charge has a qualified truth, although it reduces for the most part to the complaint which the classicist always makes of the romanticist, and begs the deeper question which is really at issue. And if 'Hernani,' for example, is rhetoric rather than poetry, as perhaps it is, what splendid rhetoric it offers its readers! When before in the French drama were 'points' ever made with such telling effect as in this melodramatic invention! 'Vous n'allez pas au fond,' 'Couvrons nous, grands d'Espagne,' 'Dieu! je suis exaucée,' 'J'en passe, et des meilleurs,' — how the examples crowd upon the memory! It may be rhetoric, but the emotions which it arouses are not readily to be distinguished from those which we experience from the purest tragic poetry.

Concerning the third charge, which makes the poet out as a person of unbounded egotism and colossal self-esteem, it may be admitted that Hugo frequently spoke of himself in terms that his truest friends might wish had been left to others to formulate. Yet modesty and self-effacement are virtues that may be carried too far, and in Hugo's case their assumption would have been a hypocritical affectation. The prophet *must* be self-conscious, else he is no prophet; he must have an exalted sense of his mission, and a fervent belief in the truth of his message. And if any nineteenth century utterance may be called prophetic, it was surely that of the man who proclaimed that

'Le poète, en des jours impies,
Vient préparer des jours meilleurs,'

and whose faith in the sacredness of his calling did not waver to the end. Posterity never condemns a man for taking the true measure of himself, even if that measure be a large one; it is only to his contemporaries, and during the period when his true dimensions are the subject of controversy, that such self-appraisal seems an act of questionable taste. When we read of Shakespeare declaring that his rhyme shall outlive 'the gilded monuments of princes,' or of Dante saying, with magnificent arrogance, — the question being of an important embassy, — 'S'io vo, chi sta; s'io sto, chi va?' we applaud rather than condemn, we admire rather than deride, the absolute conviction of the phrase. Posterity has accepted these men at their own estimates; it is more than possible that posterity may accept Hugo at his own estimate.

There are spots upon the sun — this is about the substance of what unsympathetic criticism discovers in its examination of the work of Victor Hugo. But those who all their lives have bathed in the sunlight, and felt its vivifying warmth, are content to be simply grateful, and will not, for knowledge of the sun-spots, declare the moon to be a more satisfactory orb. The positive achievement of Hugo is so immense that a volume would be needed for the barest summary. Leaving aside his miscellaneous prose, descriptive, fanciful, speculative, critical, and political, there remain the three great categories of strictly creative work, poetry, romance, and drama. This seems to be the order in which they will eventually stand, the order in which serious criticism has already placed them. To the creator of 'Hernani,' 'Ruy Blas,' and 'Marion Delorme,' we must give the credit of accomplishing the romantic revolution in French dramatic art. To the creator of 'Notre Dame de Paris,' 'Les Misérables,' and 'Quatre-vingt-treize,' we must give the credit of promulgating a new conception of the teachings of history and a new gospel of social solidarity. To the creator of 'Les Contemplations,' 'Les Châtiments,' and 'La Légende des Siècles' we must give the credit of first revealing the full singing possibilities of the French language, of rising to such a height of lyric expression as had been attained by no French poet before, of crowning the splendid edifice of French literature with its supreme revelation of pinnacled beauty. In this lyrical domain Hugo out-sang all the other poets of his age, and most of the poets of all ages; he rose as upon the pinions of the eagle, and matched the richness of Pindar; he soared as with the skylark's wings, and matched the pure note of Shelley. When at the height of his inspiration, he poured forth strains of everlasting melody, which were yet linked in thought with the noblest aspirations of the human spirit; for his genius, while ever striving after the beautiful, never forgot its allegiance to the true and the good — to the other aspects of what must ever remain the triune ideal of the soul of man.

One thing more must be said to round out this commemorative tribute to the poet whose centenary is now at hand. Of another great poet it has been written:

> 'It is indeed
> Forever well our singers should
> Utter good words and know them good
> Not through song only; with close heed
> Lest, having spent for the work's sake
> Six days, the man be left to make.'

It is 'not through song only' that we love and cherish the memory of Victor Hugo. To the

ALEXANDER THE GREAT.

'I was born,' says Alexandre Dumas, 'at Villers-Cotterets, a little town in the department of the Aisne, on the Paris road, about two hundred paces from the Rue de la Noue, where Demoustiers died, two leagues from La Ferté-Milon, where Racine was born, and seven leagues from Château-Thierry, where La Fontaine first saw the light. I was born on July 24, 1802, at half-past five in the morning, in the Rue de Lormet, in a house which now belongs to my friend Cartier, who would gladly sell it to me any day, so that I may be able to die in the very room where I was born.' As a matter of fact, he never did buy the house, but died, December 5, 1870, in a little town near Dieppe, whither he had been carried from Paris by his devoted son, on the eve of the German investment of the Capital, in order that his last days might be spared the privations of the siege. Something more than a year later, when his country was again at peace, his remains received final interment in his native town, in the presence of a famous following of authors, artists, and actors.

The bit of autobiography above quoted is characteristic at once of the geniality and the egotism of the man who wrote it. It quite takes for granted the reader's interest in every slightest personal particular that the writer may see fit to impart; it takes also for granted the reader's acceptance of the fact that neither Racine nor La Fontaine could possibly shed any greater lustre upon the region of their common birth than was shed by the author of 'Monte Cristo' and 'Les Trois Mousquetaires.' Of his own greatness, indeed, Alexandre Dumas retained an unshaken conviction throughout his long career. At the height of that career, he could assert with perfect self-assurance that for a quarter of a century past three men, Hugo, Lamartine, and himself, had remained at the head of contemporary French literature; our only marvel is that he should not have set his own name first in that trinity of literary fame. We are not of those to whom such assertions are always and necessarily classes of readers to whom literature proper makes no appeal whatever. Well do we remember the big and ugly volumes, badly printed and bound in depressing black, in which form alone the American readers of twenty or thirty years ago might make the acquaintance of d'Artagnan and Monte Cristo. Things are very different now, when tasteful editions abound, when the old-fashioned prejudices have disappeared, and when we have all of us become more or less denizens of the joyous realm of romantic invention which is still ruled by the spirit of Alexandre Dumas.

It was along in the eighties, we should say, that English and American readers of the more discriminating sort came to be attracted in considerable numbers to the romances of Dumas. Before that time, his following had been large but uncritical,—it had been a following made up for the most part of seekers for the sensational in literature, of readers who were satisfied with highly-spiced invention, and who recked little of constructive art. But Dumas really deserved a better fate than the applause of this class of readers, and he received his deserts in due course of time. It was about twenty years ago that two English critics of undeniable authority gave assurance to timid souls that their enjoyment of the French romancer was quite legitimate, and that the adventures of the three musketeers really belonged to literature. It is, we think, chiefly to Mr. Andrew Lang and Robert Louis Stevenson that the literary rehabilitation of Dumas with the English-speaking public is to be credited, for these men boldly proclaimed what many readers of taste had felt without quite daring to assert. They had coupled in thought the names of Dumas and Scott, but Mr. Lang ventured to make the conjunction on the printed page. Addressing the spirit of the Frenchman, he said:

'Than yours there has been no greater nor more kindly and beneficent force in modern letters. To Scott, indeed, you owed the first impulse of your genius; but, once set in motion, what miracles could it not accomplish? Our dear Porthos was overcome, at last, by a superhuman burden; but your imaginative strength never found a task too great for it. It is good, in a day of small and laborious ingenuities, to breathe the free air of your books, and dwell in the company of Dumas's men —so gallant, so frank, so indomitable, such swordsmen, and such trenchermen.'

This frank and generous praise is echoed by

Stevenson, who, closing his 'Vicomte de Bragelonne' after the fifth perusal, expresses his enthusiastic admiration in a series of queries which are in fact challenges to all disputants.

'What other novel has such epic variety and nobility of incident? Often, if you will, impossible; often of the order of an Arabian story; and yet all based on human nature. For if you come to that, what novel has more human nature? Not studied with the microscope, but seen largely in plain daylight, with the natural eye? What novel has more good sense, and gaiety, and wit, and unflagging, admirable literary skill? . . . And, once more, to make an end of commendations, what novel is inspired with a more unstrained or a more wholesome morality?'

These words take us far indeed from the standpoint of middle-class propriety and narrow puritanical outlook. They mark the larger and saner critical light in which our own generation has come to view the famous literature of the past.

In the presence of such tributes as these, the unlovely aspects of the character of Dumas, and the dubious aspects of his literary methods, sink into relative insignificance. Granted that he was a swaggerer and vainglorious, that petty jealousies and hypocrisies marked many stages of his career, that in his financial relations he held his personal honor too lightly; granted also that his literary *supercheries* were of unexampled audacity, that he pillaged ideas and situations from all sorts of sources, that he lent his name to books that others had written,— granted all these things, with many others of like tenor, the fact remains that he possessed an astonishingly original and prolific genius, that besides much slipshod writing that has long since been forgotten he produced a series of masterpieces that the world will not willingly let die, and that his higher ideals were on the whole ideals of manliness and clean living and devotion to admirable artistic aims.

Long before Dumas had become popular with English readers, at a time when they thought of him, so far as they thought at all, as of a writer whose stock in trade was a shallow sensationalism and a picturesque perversion of historical happenings, he was known and loved by no less a man than Thackeray, who found no difficulty in rising above English prejudice and contracting a very genuine sympathy for the most gasconading of Frenchmen. This is the language in which Thackeray deals with the vexed matter of collaboration:

'They say that all the works bearing Dumas's name are not written by him. Well? does not the chief cook have *aides* under him? Did not Rubens's pupils paint on his canvases? Had not Lawrence assistants for his backgrounds? For myself, being also *du métier*, I confess I would often like to have a competent, respectable, and rapid clerk for the business part of my novels, and on his arrival at eleven o'clock, would say, "Mr. Jones, if you please, the archbishop must die this morning in about five pages. Turn to article 'Dropsy' (or what you will) in Encyclopædia. Take care there are no medical blunders in his death. Group his daughters, physicians, and chaplains round him. In Wales's 'London,' letter B, third shelf, you will find an account of Lambeth, and some prints of the place. Colour in with local colouring. The daughter will come down and speak to her lover in his wherry at Lambeth Stairs," etc., etc. Jones (an intelligent young man) examines the medical, historical, topographical books necessary, his chief points out to him in Jeremy Taylor (fol. London, MDCLV.) a few remarks such as might befit a dear old archbishop departing this life. When I come back to dress for dinner the archbishop is dead on my table, in five pages, medicine, topography, theology, all right, and Jones has gone home to his family some hours.'

According to some such fashion as this, no doubt, much of the work of Alexandre Dumas was done, but we know as well as Thackeray did that by no such method is a trio of musketeers to be created. It is to the creative genius

Alexander the Great

that gave life to the work, however the details might be executed, that Thackeray's tribute is paid.

'Of your heroic heroes, I think our friend Monseigneur Athos, Count de la Fère, is my favorite. I have read about him from sunrise to sunset with the utmost contentment of mind. He has passed through how many volumes? Forty? Fifty? I wish, for my part, there were a hundred more, and would never tire of his rescuing prisoners, punishing ruffians, and running scoundrels through the midriff with his most graceful rapier.'

SHAKESPEARE IN FRANCE.

The learned M. Jusserand, who is as entertaining as he is learned, and who has done almost as much as Taine did (although in a very different way) to give a new interest to the history of English literature, has published a book upon the fortunes of Shakespeare among the Frenchmen. The subject of this investigation is so novel, as well as so interesting inherently, that it seems worth while to tell M. Jusserand's story in condensed form, although it has been made fully accessible to English readers. Of course, we all know in its general outline the history of Shakespearian study in France, but few even among students know the interesting details of the narrative which M. Jusserand has illustrated from the wealth of his rich and curious reading, which he has adorned with his piquant style and warmed with his sympathetic 'appreciation' of the greatest poet of the modern world.

M. Jusserand introduces his narrative by setting

side by side two passages, published respectively in 1645 and 1765, and roughly indicating the limits of the period to which the chief interest of the story attaches, the period during which Shakespeare won his way to the French consciousness. The first extract is from Blaeu's 'Théâtre du Monde,' a sort of glorified gazeteer, and informs the reader that Stratford is a pleasant little town which owes its entire glory to 'Jehan de Stratford, archevêque de Cantorbéry' and 'Hugues de Clopton, juge à Londres.' One of these worthies, it seems, built a church in Stratford, and the other spanned the Avon with a bridge. To this writer, Shakespeare was less than a name; Stratford had enough of glory in its claim upon the primate and the judge. The other extract is from the 'Encyclopædia,' and speaks of Stratford in this fashion: 'It was not long ago that the house in which Shakespeare (William) died in 1616 was still pointed out in this town; it was even regarded as a curiosity of the country and the inhabitants regretted its destruction, so jealous are they of the glory of having given birth to this sublime genius, the greatest in all dramatic poetry.' The article fills five columns, and although its title is 'Stratford,' its exclusive subject is Shakespeare. To trace the history of the change in French opinion thus brought about by a century has been the task of M. Jusserand, and the subject is one richly deserving of attention.

The first judgment upon Shakespeare to find expression in the French language occurs in a catalogue of the Royal Library (1675–1684). A copy of the second folio had found its way into the collection, and the entry of the cataloguer included, besides a Latinized form of the title, the following note: 'This English poet has a rather fine imagination, he thinks naturally, he expresses himself with delicacy, but these fine qualities are darkened by the filth that he mingles with his comedies.' An inventory of Fouquet's library shows that it also contained a volume of Shakespeare 'valued at one livre.' The first *printed* mention of Shakespeare in France occurs in Baillet's 'Jugements des Savants' (1685–6). Here the name is given, without comment, in a list of English poets. Two or three other fugitive allusions to a poet variously named 'Shakspear' and 'Shakees Pear' may be found during the closing years of the reign of the Roi-Soleil, but the great age of French literature was over, and Corneille, Racine, and Molière had long been in their graves, before even a Frenchman here and there had so much as dreamed that the English poet who had died when Corneille was a boy of ten was destined to enjoy a heritage of fame so world-wide and so enduring that even the genius of Molière would come to seem pale in the comparison.

The first half of the eighteenth century changed all this. Not only did Shakespeare become widely known in France, through criticism and even through translation, but his plays began to influence the French stage, and to awaken an uneasy feeling that possibly the rules of the classic drama might not have said the final word upon the subject of dramatic composition. During the period in question a great many writers found occasion to speak of Shakespeare in appreciative terms, and some of these writers were men whose opinions carried much weight. The Abbé Prévost, who made a long stay in England, and began to publish his 'Mémoires' in 1728, became a genuine anglomaniac, the first in date

knowledge of the rules.' In the introduction to
'Sémiramis' (1748), where the famous epithet
of the 'drunken savage' occurs, he said that
'Hamlet' contains 'sublime strokes worthy of
the loftiest geniuses. It seems as if nature had
taken delight in collecting within the brain of
Shakespeare all that we can imagine of what is
greatest and most powerful, with all that rudeness
without wit can contain of what is lowest and
most detestable.' Testimonies to Shakespeare
were now rapidly multiplying. Riccoboni (1738)
wrote a history of the English stage, saying of
Shakespeare that 'having used up his patrimony,
he took up the trade of robber. He wrote san-
guinary dramas, "Hamlet" among others, and
"Othello," in which we witness the incredible
strangling of Desdemona.' Le Blanc (1745)
found fairly fitting words in which to express the
magic of Shakespeare's style. Finally, La Place
(1746) made a French translation of many of the
plays, and prepared analyses of the others.

In the latter half of the eighteenth century, we
come face to face with the 'Shakespeare question,' which fills the last and most interesting
chapter in all this curious history. Speaking of

the translation of 'Tom Jones' made in 1750, d'Argenson remarked: 'Anglicism is gaining upon us,' while Boissy, in a comedy dated 1753, made sport of the fickle tastes of the French public, which sought after strange gods, now in Italy, now in England.

> 'Son transport l'autre jour était l'anglomanie;
> Rien sans l'habit anglais ne pouvait réussir;
> Au-dessus de Corneille il mettait Shakespir.'

Something clearly had to be done, and Voltaire, who felt that both his critical precept and his practice as a dramatic poet had been largely responsible for this exaltation of the 'sauvage ivre,' stepped into the breach. It was all very well to praise Shakespeare in measured terms, as he had himself done, but when it came to a complete and sumptuous translation, dedicated to the king, and prefaced by the judgment that 'never had man of genius penetrated deeper into the abyss of the human heart or given better and more natural speech to the passions,' it was really going too far. 'Had not he [Voltaire] granted enough to the monster? Had not he introduced certain liberties to the French stage? Had not he cleared, and pruned, and given regular shape

THE TIE THAT BINDS.

THE beautiful story of the Athenian captives at Syracuse, set free and restored with all honors to their fatherland because they could recite verses from the poet best beloved of their captors, has been made familiar to us all by two among the noblest works of Robert Browning. 'Any such happy man had prompt reward,' our poet tells us,

'If he lay bleeding on the battle-field
They stanched his wounds, and gave him drink and food;
If he were slave i' the house, for reverence
They rose up, bowed to who proved master now,
And bade him go free, thank Euripides!
Ay, and such did so: many such, he said,
Returning home to Athens, sought him out,
The old bard in the solitary house,
And thanked him ere they went to sacrifice.'

This story has much more than the virtue of an anecdote; it has rather the significance of an eternal truth, of the everlasting power of literature to reconcile differences, to soften the asperities of intercourse between nations, to strengthen the bonds of sympathy between human beings, and to

The Tie That Binds

offer promise of that 'Parliament of man, the Federation of the world,' which the poet still insists upon foreseeing, however idle his dream be held by the reluctant and short-sighted multitude.

While the vision of the seer halts at nothing short of this ideal of the brotherhood of man finally accomplished, he whose faith is less firm and whose gaze cannot descry things hidden so deep in the mists of the future may still find in the possession of a common speech some earnest of a harmonious union for all to whom that speech is native. Particularly true is this of us born to the use of the English language,

> 'Who speak the tongue
> That Shakespeare spake, the faith and morals hold
> Which Milton held.'

A common language is the tie that binds men together almost in spite of themselves. This is true even if the language be one that has never risen to supreme excellence of expression upon the lips of the literary artist. A striking illustration of this fact is offered by Miss Olive Schreiner, in her account of the uncouth *Taal* of the Boer. The Boer himself is of mixed Dutch and Huguenot strain, and his speech is an almost inconceivably degraded dialect of the Dutch tongue. It is absolutely without a literature, and is probably incapable of originating one. Yet it has fused into a compact nationality the heterogeneous elements that went to the making of the Boer, and its unifying influence compels our admiration and our respect. If this be the power of a rough and poverty-stricken dialect, what limits may be set to the potency of so rich and refined an instrument of intercourse as the English language? It is not from mere pride of race that the philosophical observer rejoices in the amazing spread of the English language over the face of the earth. It is rather that he feels the immense significance to the future of mankind that must attach to an ever-widening use of the tongue in whose literature are embodied the noblest civic and ethical ideals of the modern world.

Ten generations have now followed one another since the man who in English speech gave supreme expression to these ideals was with us in the flesh. It is three centuries since the gentlest, and wisest, and deepest of modern souls was building the monument of song that none knew better than himself 'would outlive the perishing

The Tie That Binds

body of men and things till the Resurrection of the Dead.' And who will dare say that the work of Shakespeare is more than barely begun? Year after year we commemorate the anniversary of his birth, and each year we look back with reverence to the past because of the promise that it gives us for the future. The words spoken a few years ago at the Stratford celebration by the man who so worthily represented among the English people the best elements of American culture, and the message of good-will sent to the Birmingham gathering by the Chief Magistrate of our Republic, were both expressions of the feeling that a common claim to Shakespeare constitutes between England and the United States a bond of union too strong to be broken by differences that might cause other nations to fly at one another's throats, too sacred to be made the sport of political passion or weakened by petty international jealousies.

The Philistine, we suppose, smiled at Mr. Cleveland's message, deeming it a bit of ineffectual but harmless sentimentality, yet the message embodied a deeper truth than ever entered into the self-satisfied Philistine consciousness.

Doubtless, also, he smiled at Mr. Bayard's assertion that America claimed Shakespeare no less than England, yet that too is the deepest kind of a truth. There is much reason to believe that the teaching of American history in our public schools leaves dominant in the child's mind an impression that England is our hereditary enemy. How much better it would be, and how much more essentially just, to emphasize the fact that, although temporary differences have now and then arisen between the two nations, yet these are as nothing in comparison with the glory of their common inheritance; that English history, from Alfred to Cromwell, belongs to us as rightfully as to our kinsmen over-sea, and should be to us a source of no less pride than that we justly take in the continuation of the history through Washington down to Lincoln. That this is the view ultimately to obtain among the English-speaking peoples seems to us certain. The very stars in their courses are working to bring it about, and the quiet, irresistible influence of a common intellectual tradition will some day accomplish a closer and more vital union between the scattered sections of the English family than was ever cemented by bond of dynasty or political organization in the history of the world. There is a larger patriotism than that of the state, a wider fellowship than that of the geographical area; it is in community of achievement and aspiration that men are in truth brothers, and it is in literature that they find their real relationship.

The mutterings of war between the two great English-speaking peoples not long ago called forth by a reckless play in the politico-diplomatic game have not been wholly evil in their effect. If they were accompanied by a melancholy display of truculence on the part of time-serving politicians and journalists, they also served to make clear the almost absolute unanimity of the better elements of English-speaking society in rejecting the thought of such a war as a horror unspeakable and unthinkable. That it would be essentially civil war was the general verdict of sober-minded observers, for the essential characteristic of civil war is that the opposing forces should be sharers of the same sympathies and ideals, whether sharing or not the same governmental machinery. If all civilized nations knew each other as well as the sections of the English race know each other, all war would be civil war, and burdened with the awful responsibilities of such strife. The jingoes and the fomenters of international ill-feeling are poor prophets. We prefer to pin our faith to the prophecy of the distinguished Englishman who once spoke to the members of the Harvard Law School. Upon that occasion, Sir Frederick Pollock, discussing 'The Vocation of the Common Law,' brought his remarks to a close with a peroration so significant and so eloquent that we cannot resist the temptation to borrow it for the adornment of our own discussion of so nearly allied a theme. 'Dreams are not versed in issuable matter, and have no dates. Only I feel that this one looks forward, and will be seen as waking light some day. If anyone, being of little faith or over-curious, must needs ask in what day, I can answer only in the same fashion. We may know the signs, though we know not when they will come. These things will be when we look back on our dissensions in the past as brethren grown up to man's estate and dwelling in unity look back upon the bickerings of the nursery and the jealousies of the class-room; when there is no use for the word "foreigner" between Cape Wrath and the Rio Grande, and the federated navies of the English-speaking nations keep the peace of the ocean under the Northern Lights and under the Southern Cross, from Vancouver to Sydney, and from the Channel to the Gulf of Mexico; when an indestructible union of even wider grasp and higher potency than the federal bond of these States has knit our descendants into an invincible and indestructible concord.'

INTERNATIONAL AMITY.

A FULL generation has now passed since the publication of 'The Coming Race,' by the versatile novelist who had given us books as various as 'Pelham,' 'A Strange Story,' 'Harold,' 'The Caxtons,' and 'Kenelm Chillingly.' This forecast was impressive in many ways, but in no way more impressive than in its assertion that war would eventually be made impossible through improvements in the means of destruction. Weapons would become so deadly that war would practically mean annihilation of the contending forces, and the good sense of the nations would prevail in the abandonment of this barbaric way of settling disputes. The past thirty years have witnessed, not exactly the literal fulfillment of this prediction, but marked progress in the direction of its fulfillment, and, as a natural consequence of the increased effectiveness of fighting instruments, a marked reluctance to resort to the arbitrament of war.

International Amity

Within much more recent years, a great Russian authority upon the art of war, as well as a man of the widest experience in practical affairs, has argued with convincing logic that war is fast becoming a practical impossibility. This beneficent result of scientific progress is due, not simply, as in Bulwer's argument, because of the increasing deadliness of weapons, but rather because, with this increasing deadliness, the advantage to the defense becomes so much greater than the advantage to the attack that all wars of the ordinary type, in which an invading army seeks to conquer a foreign country, must henceforth be so hopelessly one-sided as to be entirely futile. The position of the late M. de Bloch has received ample confirmation during the course of the distressing struggles of late years, in South Africa and the Philippine Islands, and the lesson of these conflicts is not likely to be missed. Entirely aside from the moral issues involved, both of these wars have borne out the essential assertion of M. de Bloch that a small body of men, armed with the modern means of defense, can resist, for an indefinite period, an invading body of overwhelmingly superior strength. In making this principle one memorable thing about it, and will be likely to influence the relations between Germany and America for many years to come. The visit will remain a gracious memory long after the glitter of the event shall have grown dim in our recollection.

Another recent event of similar significance was the visit of the Baron d'Estournelles de Constant, bearing the greetings of the great European Republic to its sister Republic in the West. This distinguished statesman, journeying from Paris to Chicago for the express purpose of paying a Frenchman's tribute to the memory of the greatest of Americans, pleaded in eloquent terms for the cause of international good-will, for the sinking of political jealousies and commercial rivalries in the larger interests of the common humanity of the race, and wherever he spoke his noble idealism — which is nevertheless that of a practical man of the world — aroused echoes of responsive sympathy in the breasts of his hearers. Now the influence which is represented by such visits as these, and supplemented by the many other modern agencies which tend to the creation of a mutual understanding between our own people and those of a foreign country, amounts in the

International Amity

total sum to an incalculably great force exerted in the interests of civilization and for the removal of ancient prejudice. Whenever men are brought together on the basis of a common interest, whether intellectual or social, the racial barriers first raised between them are at once cast down, and are as if they had never existed. Every international gathering of men of politics, of science, or of literature, offers a silent but effective protest against the passions which set nations at war with one another.

We do not expect that the world will be swayed by reason alone for many generations yet. Nevertheless, the ascendancy of reason is by slow degrees making itself felt. In spite of all discouragements, 'man is being made,' in Tennyson's phrase, and

'Prophet-eyes may catch a glory slowly gaining on the shade.'

To the logical mind the outcome of the evolutionary process, however long-delayed, is sure. Such a mind must admit that even patriotism is selfishness, although at several removes from what we commonly call by that name. There is the selfishness of the individual, first of all, which has should seek more earnestly than at another to be delivered from all prejudice, error, and weakness, it is when he essays the role of the hero-maker. If he fails in this, he may well question if all the other good he may have accomplished has not been over-balanced. There is a mawkish notion prevalent among the members of a certain very advanced class of people in almost all parts of the world, that if you add cant to crime you lessen the crime. Some of them think that the outcome of such a combination is the most heroic virtue. All of us judge crime more leniently when committed by persons who have views in common with us upon some important subject, and against persons whom we regard with feelings of hostility. But the moralist, the historian, and the inventor of epics are under bonds to civilization to rise above such weakness.'

The false kind of sentiment that is here condemned in such impressive terms has done much mischief in perverting the ethical judgments passed by mankind upon the conspicuous figures of history. In ancient times, it deified Alexander the Great and Julius Cæsar, to say nothing of a long line of lesser conquerors and leaders of vic-

Hero-Worship

torious hosts. In our own century, it has made of Napoleon a subject for eulogy rather than for execration, it has in a measure justified the career of the man of 'blood and iron' who looms so large in the history of modern Germany, and it has recently been engaged in glossing over the unscrupulous methods of the ambitious adventurer who came to regard South Africa as his own personal appanage. It would seem, indeed, when we consider these and the many similar cases which history presents to our view, that success, by whatever means achieved, is too often taken by the public as the adequate test of greatness, and that a man's career passes for heroic if only it be sufficiently brilliant to attract widespread attention, and sufficiently daring to impose upon the imagination of men. The ethical philosopher, of course, bases his judgment upon other criteria than these, for he knows that failure is often more heroic than success, and that many a mute inglorious career, with which only the few are acquainted, may offer a finer example for the emulation of mankind than is offered by the lives of those who shine in the fierce light that beats upon the seats of the mighty.

Carlyle has done much to glorify the type of man who succeeds by sheer strength of will, and the gospel of brute force has collected a singular company in his gallery of heroic figures. Yet it is from Carlyle himself that we have chosen a passage which emphasizes, better than it has often been emphasized, the eternal distinction between the strength that should command our admiration and the strength that is perversely employed. 'A certain strong man, of former time, fought stoutly at Lepanto; worked stoutly as Algerine slave; stoutly delivered himself from such working; with stout cheerfulness endured famine and nakedness and the world's ingratitude; and sitting in jail, with the one arm left him, wrote our joyfullest, and all but our deepest, modern book, and named it "Don Quijote": this was a genuine strong man. A strong man, of recent time, fights little for any good cause anywhere; works weakly as an English lord; weakly delivers himself from such working; with weak despondency endures the cackling of plucked geese at St. James; and, sitting in sunny Italy, in his coach-and-four, at a distance of two thousand miles from them, writes, over many reams of paper, the following sentence, with variations: "Saw ever the world one greater or unhappier?" This was a sham strong man. Choose ye.' While this comparison, in its straining for antithetical effects, is not altogether fair to Byron, whose life was at least closed by a piece of genuine heroism, yet in the main it enforces a lesson that should be taken to heart. The Byronic cult was undoubtedly in its day responsible for a great deal of sickly sentimentalism, and its influence still lingers in English literature. As contrasted with Shelley's ardent and high-souled devotion to great causes and fine ideals, the passion of Byron at its best seems theatrical and insincere, and the gospel of 'Childe Harold' is but a poor thing when viewed in the glowing light of the ' Prometheus Unbound.'

In literature, as in other departments of human activity, there are sham heroes as well as genuine ones. This statement is not meant to imply that a writer whose private life will not bear the closest scrutiny is for that reason unheroic as a literary figure, for the weakness of will by which personal conduct is so often misshapen may coëxist with an intellectual life of the rarest distinction. And since the essential thing about a writer is his work, he has a right to be judged by that work, almost irrespective of the life that lies behind it. The figure of Schopenhauer, for example, is one of the most heroic in literature, although the character of the man, as apart from the writer, left much to be desired. But the noble sincerity of his work, and its exaltation of fine ideals in both thought and conduct, are qualities so marked that we are quite justified in ignoring the unlovely aspects of the personal biography. On the other hand, the most conspicuous of literary figures may fail to assume heroic proportions if the work for which it stands have any suggestion of pose or insincerity. We may be very indulgent to the infirmities of the flesh, provided only they do not fetter or drag down the spirit. There is a false ring, which no sounding rhetoric can altogether deaden to the discerning ear, in the work of many masterful writers, and when that ring is once detected, the power of the voice to shape our intellectual ideals becomes sadly weakened. This false note may be caught over and over again in Byron; it makes the Whitman cult seem a strange phenomenon to minds entirely well-balanced and sane, and it lessens the effective appeal of even such giants as Hugo and Carlyle.

When we think of certain figures in literature as peculiarly heroic, we do not usually stop for analysis, but are content to rest the judgment upon a mixture of impressions, in part derived from the life, and in part from the work. Scott and Balzac are good examples of this, for both are heroic figures in a very genuine sense, and we hardly know whether to admire them the more for their courageous struggle against adverse material conditions or for their resolute pursuit of a great creative purpose. Instead of taking these men for our illustration, let us take instead a man who was a hero of literature pure and simple, a man whose career has for the literary worker the same sort of lessons that the career of Spinoza has for the philosopher, of Gordon for the soldier, or of Mazzini for the statesman. The man is Gustave Flaubert, and our task is made easy by borrowing from an eloquent address made at Oxford by M. Paul Bourget. 'No man was ever more richly endowed with the higher virtues of a great literary artist,' says M. Bourget.

'His whole existence was one long struggle against circumstances and against himself, to live up to that ideal standard as a writer which he had set before himself from his earliest years. . . . He remains ever present among us, in spite of the new developments assumed by contemporary French literature, for he gave to all writers the most splendid example of passionate, exclusive love of literature. With his long years of patient and scrupulous toil, his noble contempt of wealth, honours, and popularity, with his courage in pursuing to the end the realization of his dream, he looms upon us an intellectual hero.'

And yet with all his passion for the impersonal, with all his striving to view life from the outside, holding, or at least expressing, 'no form of creed, but contemplating all,' the final lesson of Flaubert's life is, as his eulogist admits, that no man may wholly exclude himself from his writings. Had the author of 'Madame Bovary' really done so, 'they would not have reached us all imbued with that melancholy savour, that subdued pathos which makes them so dear to us. . . . This gift of expressing in their writings more than they themselves suspect, and of achieving results exceeding their ambition, is only granted to those courageous and sincere geniuses whose past trials have gained for them the priceless treasure of wide experience. Thus did Cervantes write "Don Quijote," and Defoe "Robinson Crusoe," little dreaming that they infused into their writings, the former all the glowing heroism of Spain, the latter the dogged self-reliance of the Anglo-Saxon. If they had not themselves for many years practised these virtues of chivalrous enterprise in the one case, of indomitable endurance in the other, their books would have been what they intended them to be — mere tales of adventure. But their souls were greater than their art, and imbued it throughout with that symbolic power which is the efficient vitality of books. In the same way Flaubert's soul was greater than his art, and it is that soul which, in spite of his own will, he breathed into his writings, gaining for them a place apart in the history of the contemporary French novel.' Thus we come back, after all, to the position that heroism in literary production is somehow the outcome or reflex of something heroic in the character and the temper of the writer. It may be only a streak, so blended with others as to be almost undiscernible to observers of the man apart from his books, yet it is the deepest and truest part of him, and a noble book of any sort may well give pause to the judgment that too hastily condemns a man's life because it is visibly flawed. But those men are the fittest subjects for hero-worship in whom the life and the word are the most fully consonant, whose lives are poems, and whose words are acts. Such a hero was Goethe, with his lifelong devotion to the ideal that held the whole of life to be even more important than its separate elements of the good and the beautiful; such was Milton, whose 'soul was like a star, and dwelt apart,' and yet whose heart 'the lowliest duties on herself did lay'; such was Dante, whose exiled soul still 'possessed the sun and stars,' and whose divine poem was wrought not as a poem merely, but

> 'With close heed
> Lest, having spent for the work's sake
> Six days, the man be left to make.'

A PHILISTINE WATCHWORD.

READERS of 'The International Journal of Ethics' must have rubbed their eyes when they received a certain number of that earnest and valuable review, and found its first score of pages devoted to the great achievement of Dr. Nansen in Arctic exploration. What has such a matter to do with ethics? they may well have asked, and why should our attention be diverted to the deeds of this hardy Norseman when all our intellectual energies are needed for the examination of such engaging subjects as 'the relation of pessimism to ultimate philosophy,' and 'our social and ethical solidarity,' and 'the history and spirit of Chinese ethics,' to instance a few of the themes discussed within the same covers. The fact that Mr. Leslie Stephen was responsible for this diversion gave promise, indeed, of a high degree of intellectual entertainment; but one had to get well along into the essay before discovering what Dr. Nansen was really doing in this galley. The name of the chiefly to those who have consciously labored to redress grievances and remove causes of misery, but to men who have pursued intellectual aims, scientific or artistic, for the pure love of art or science.' And he concludes by saying that 'the true doctrine seems to be that it is an imperative duty for a man to devote his intellect to those purposes, whatever they may be, to which it is most fitted.'

The spokesmen of the 'practical' have done so much in all ages, and are still doing so much, to chill enthusiasms and to narrow the scope of life, that we make no apology for recurring to this well-worn theme, and pointing out once more the essential misconception of those well-intentioned but purblind persons. 'Why was this waste of the ointment made?' is a question that we hear repeated, in various disguises, every day of our lives. Now there are two satisfactory answers to the question in all of its forms: one of them faces the utilitarian critic upon his own plane and leaves him no ground upon which to stand, while the other makes the radical demand that he broaden his conception of utility and rearrange his notions of conduct in accordance with a far

A QUESTION OF LITERARY CONSCIENCE.

THERE are few chapters of literary criticism that surpass, in display of subtle insight and essential justice of conclusion, the well-known essay of Charles Lamb upon the artificial comedy of the Restoration. This essay has always been a stumbling-block to the Philistine, and will always appear paradoxical to the reader whose intellectual perceptions do not nicely balance his moral prepossessions. Macaulay, as we know, found it both a paradox and a stumbling-block, and assailed it with the weaver's beam that he wielded with such redoubtable energy. But in spite of the attack of Macaulay, and of other persons defective in their literary sympathies, the ideas advanced by Lamb in this essay have held their own, and criticism has accepted their fundamental validity. It will be remembered that Lamb's argument runs, in substance, to the effect that the writers whom he defends created a conventional world of their own, in which the rules that ordinarily govern, and properly should govern, human conduct, have no more application than the rules of ordinary probability to the incidents of a Grimm *Mährchen* or an Arabian tale. Lamb declared himself 'glad for a season to take an airing beyond the diocese of the strict conscience,' and now and then 'for a dream-while or so, to imagine a world with no meddling restrictions.' The world of Congreve and Wycherley 'is altogether a speculative scene of things, which has no reference whatever to the world that is. . . . The whole is a passing pageant, where we should sit as unconcerned at the issues, for life or death, as at a battle of the frogs and mice.' His complaint is that people no longer take delight in the pageant, because they have grown too strenuous in their literal-minded interpretation of the show. 'Like Don Quixote, we take part against the puppets, and quite as impertinently.' We are too self-conscious to give ourselves up to mere distraction, and go to the theatre not 'to escape from the pressure of reality so much as to confirm our experience of it; to make assurance double, and take a bond of fate.'

A Question of Conscience

The fashion of the Restoration comedy is one that has now passed away from popular interest, but another fashion has taken its place, concerning which Lamb's argument is equally to the point. This is the fashion of romantic fiction, toward which our strenuous moralists are apt to assume a deprecatory attitude, upon much the same grounds that served as a basis for the condemnation of the earlier fashion. Romantic fiction is essentially unreal, we are told; it does not reflect the conditions of actual life, it encourages us to dream instead of setting us face to face with the problems of human existence, it dissipates our energies instead of enlisting them in behalf of worthy social and intellectual causes. The charge is doubtless true, but is there no place for dreams in the economy of the spiritual life? Are we to reject the ministry of every form of literature that takes us away from our surroundings, or is not closely related to our immediate pursuits and interests? Entertainment may not be the highest mission of literature, but it is surely a legitimate object for a writer to set before himself, and those writers who offer entertainment, in whatever fashion the hour may approve, are not undeserving of the public and will not find their efforts unrewarded. To say that romantic fiction moves in an unreal world of its own making should not be held a matter for reproach; it should rather be recognized as the necessary condition of this form of art, and should make us grateful for the refuge which it offers to the mind oppressed by the burden, at times so intolerable, of the actual world. The art of fiction depends upon conventions quite as fully as does the dramatic art. The action must be compressed far beyond the limits of probability, and worked out with small regard for the many disturbing influences by which it would certainly be complicated in real life. The villain must be foiled, the hero must triumph, and the lovers must be united, even if there are only a score of pages in which to accomplish all these things. Whatever the length of the story, these are its fundamental requirements; and to such ends all the means employed by the writer must be bent. Each separate scene, moreover, must be heightened in effect far beyond anything that is likely to occur in everyday life; two people seated side by side at a dinner-table must make their conversation more brilliant than any that was ever actually heard upon such an occasion; the members of every group of persons brought into contact for the purposes of the narrative must say and do just the right things at the right moments, instead of floundering about in act and speech as they doubtless would in the haphazard actual world. In that world, as the poet reminds us, we get 'never the time and the place and the loved one all together'; but in the world which the romantic imagination creates we have a right to expect this conjunction, and a reason for justifiable disappointment if it is missed.

The romance of pure adventure appeals to some of our healthiest instincts. Both as boys and as men, we like to follow the fortunes of pirates, to read about shipwrecks and all other sorts of forlorn hopes, and to applaud the deeds of heroes who slay their enemies right and left, and escape from the most desperate dangers by feats of improbable prowess and display of indomitable if not superhuman valor. The gentlest spirits as well as the most fiery delight in these things, and delight in them precisely because they are so far removed from ordinary human experience. They are the happenings of a world which, at least when we have outgrown boyhood, we have no desire to make our own, a world which could not be our own if we wished it, a world which we frankly recognize as imagined for our diversion. We should ill requite those who purvey for us all this innocent entertainment were we to arraign them before the bar of conscience, to make stern inquiry into the probability of their imaginings, and to pronounce upon the conduct of their characters such severe judgments as would doubtless await such conduct in the courts of justice of our prosaic world.

Nevertheless, although we are fully persuaded of the right of romantic fiction to exist and of its heroes to perform acts which would not bear the test of a prosaic and conventional morality, we are not without certain searchings of soul when we contemplate the enormous vogue enjoyed by this species of literature at the present day. Of that vogue there can be no question. It would be difficult to point to any earlier period in which popular fiction was so largely made up of tales of adventure, tales whose interest centres upon exploits rather than principles, upon the triumph of the individual will rather than of the abstract ideal. There is an appalling amount of bloodshed in our popular romance, and an almost unexampled degree of recklessness in the choice of means for the desired end. One need not be a professional moralist to correlate this illustration of popular taste with the wave of brutality which seems to be sweeping over our civilization, and which threatens to submerge the moral territory that has been reclaimed at so great a cost of individual and collective effort. For some reason or other, the finer instincts of civilization seem of late years to have become dulled, and both individuals and nations are suffered without effective protest to commit acts which should arouse the fiercest indignation for their contravention of all the principles by which nations achieve true greatness and individuals bequeath to their descendants a heritage of honorable fame. We should hardly include our popular literature among the active causes of this degenerative process, but it may not be unfair to regard it as symptomatic. We may read with zest the popular literature which glories in brute force, and we may get no harm from it as individuals; but we must 'view with alarm,' as the political platforms say, the ever-increasing hold which this species of literature is gaining upon the popular mind. If such literature does not directly shape the actions of men, it certainly does to some extent reflect their ideals, and its present prominence is such as to confront the literary conscience with a serious question. Should we, because they afford us such admirable entertainment, give our unqualified approval to these writings that glorify all the brutal passions, that move in a world unswayed by the moral law, and that substitute for the Christian precepts a gospel whereof Carlyle and Nietzsche are the evangelists? It is a serious question, whether the ideals of public and private morality, as reflected in the popular literature of the day, which the century has just passed on to the present, will bear a favorable comparison with those which were bequeathed to the last century by its predecessor.

THE ARTIST AND THE MAN.

AMONG the many principles for which the late John Ruskin contended with all the force of his impassioned and vehement eloquence, there is one which occupies a peculiarly significant position. It is the principle that a man's art and a man's character are so mutually dependent that the latter is implicit in the former. This principle is central in the great critic's doctrine, for it supplies the nexus whereby his ethics and his æsthetics become united into a single body of teaching. It affords the justification for his constant injection of moral questions into his discussions of art, and for his persistent employment of artistic illustrative material in his treatment of the problems that relate to the conduct of life. The principle in question finds its typical expression in such sentences as these: 'The faults of a work of art are the faults of its workman, and its virtues his virtues.' 'Great art is the expression of the mind of a great man, and it gives us a sense of satisfaction to take refuge in even the extreme opinion that poetry has no business to teach anything, that its message is one of pure beauty, and that, by just so much as it departs from this aim, its purpose becomes weakened, and its spiritual power impaired. The second reason which seemed to justify the principle of 'art for art's sake' was offered by those over-zealous critics of literature who were constantly dragging petty personalities into their work, raising a great pother over the superficial aspects of a poet's private life, and making out of some carelessness of habit or fault of temper a structural defect in character which must always be kept in the foreground of thought when the poet's work was under consideration. It was no wonder that these two influences combined drove many sensitive intelligences to the extreme of revolt. The fact that, on the one hand, such didacticism as Young's 'Night Thoughts' and Pollok's 'Course of Time' could pass for poetry at all, and that, on the other, whole sections of the reading public should be warned against the poetry of Byron and Shelley because their lives did not square with the social conventions of their time — this twofold fact, we say, based upon a false perspective and a complete misunderstanding of the poetic art, was amply sufficient to account for the success of a form of teaching whose fundamental object was to restore to poetry the dignity which it seemed to be in danger of losing.

When, however, we come to take a broader view of the whole question, it must be admitted that the doctrine of 'art for art's sake,' the doctrine that the artist must deliberately eschew the intention of teaching, that, if he have the divine fire within him, the purity of its glow will remain undimmed whatever the life he may lead, is almost as narrow as the doctrine against which it was raised in protest. Because certain dull poets have been offensively didactic we have no right to say that poets of genius may not engage their powers in the furtherance of worthy ideals. That some great poets have had personal failings, about which their critics have been more curious than was necessary, is no reason why we should deny that, other things being equal, the blameless life will in the long run express itself in nobler forms than the life that has not escaped 'the give each other the lie, why should we jump to the conclusion that the written expression of character must be insincere; why not take the more reasonable view that the true personality is to be sought in the books? They, at least, if read aright, offer a form of self-expression that is deliberate and clear; while a man's daily actions are impulsive and open to a hundred misinterpretations.

Again writing of Milton, Professor Corson says: 'His personality is felt in his every production, poetical and prose, and felt almost as much in the earliest as in the latest period of his authorship. And there is no epithet more applicable to his own personality than the epithet august. He is therefore one of the most educating of authors, in the highest sense of the word, that is, educating in the direction of sanctified character.' What is here said of Milton we believe to be equally true of Shakespeare. We all know what Wordsworth said of the sonnet, that 'with this key Shakespeare unlocked his heart,' how Browning replied to this dictum with an indignant, 'If so, the less Shakespeare he,' and how Matthew Arnold, in a vein similar to that of Browning, wrote these lines:

> 'Others abide our question. Thou art free.
> We ask and ask — Thou smilest and art still,
> Out-topping knowledge.'

In this conflict of opinion, it seems to us that Wordsworth has expressed the deeper truth. It is true that the closest scrutiny of Shakespeare's work will not give us the facts about his boyish poaching upon Sir Thomas Lucy's preserves, or explain the mystery of that 'second-best bed' bequeathed to his wife. But the knowledge of a man's personality does not depend upon such trivialities as these. We know his qualities of heart and mind better than we know those of our closest friends. We know what he thought upon most serious subjects, and how he felt about human life in its most significant aspects. The superstition which would have us believe that, as a dramatist, he exhibited the personalities of his created characters and concealed his own beyond any possibility of surmise has been tenacious, but is at last losing its hold upon intelligent students. The little book of Mr.

Frank Harris upon the man Shakespeare, and the still more recent book of Professor Goldwin Smith upon the same subject, are interesting records of the change of opinion upon this subject. Still more interesting is the closing paragraph of the important work of Shakespearian criticism which we owe to Dr. Brandes:

'The William Shakespeare who was born at Stratford-on-Avon in the reign of Queen Elizabeth, who lived and wrote in London in her reign and that of James, who ascended into heaven in his comedies and descended into hell in his tragedies, and died at the age of fifty-two in his native town, rises a wonderful personality in grand and distinct outlines, with all the vivid coloring of life from the pages of his books, before the eyes of all who read them with an open, receptive mind, with sanity of judgment, and simple susceptibility to the power of genius.'

THE DUTIES OF AUTHORS.

THAT every right implies a correlated duty, and that the assertion of the one should be conditioned upon the acceptance of the other, is a principle in which theoretical is more common than practical acquiescence. The burden of Mazzini's criticism of the French Revolution was that it gave undue prominence to the Rights of Man, and had little to say about the corresponding Duties of Man. It was the fundamental aim of that patient, heroic soul to moralize the European revolutionary movement by insisting upon the claim of duty as a necessary accompaniment of the claim of right.

Transferring the discussion from the political to the literary plane, we are inclined to think that too much has lately been heard about the rights of authors in comparison with what is said about their duties. It is then with peculiar satisfaction that we call attention to the chapter on 'The Duties of Authors' included in Mr.

Leslie Stephen's collection of addresses to ethical societies. While Sir Walter Besant and his associates in the Society of Authors are engaged in the praiseworthy work of exposing the wily ways of the dishonest publisher, it is well that a strong voice should now and then discourse upon the responsibilities of authorship, and sound a note of warning against the temptations which beset the man of letters under the modern commercial literary *régime*. The ethics of literature is a large subject with many ramifications, and neither Mr. Stephen nor any other man could hope to treat of it exhaustively within the limits of a single essay; but the address to which reference is now made touches upon the more salient features of the subject, and is characterized in unusual measure by good sense, sound logic, and fine ethical tone.

So large a proportion of literary energy nowadays is absorbed by journalism that no discussion of the duties of authors can ignore the work of those who write for the newspaper press. It is in journalism, also, that writers are most strongly assailed by the temptations peculiar to their craft. The question of anonymity, for

The Duties of Authors

example, is one that must be considered in its ethical relations, and it takes the keenest self-searching for a man to be sure that under the impersonal shelter of the plural pronoun he is not saying things to which he would blush to attach his signature. Nothing is more contemptible than the work of the writer who makes himself a hireling of some party organ, and earns his daily bread by the advocacy of doctrines to which he does not personally subscribe; doctrines that are abhorrent to him as an individual. Such a prostitution of literary talent may be defended, is defended, in many ingenious ways, but the cobwebs of sophistry woven about the discussion by defenders of this practice are easily swept away by anyone who is determined to see things as they are and regulate his conduct in accordance with the fundamental principles of morality. The stock argument by which lawyers justify their defence of the criminal of whose guilt they are convinced — the plea that such a person is entitled to the most favorable interpretation of which the law admits, and that someone must secure it for him — is not valid in the discussion of questions of public interest. No matter of governmental policy is entitled to any other defence than may be made for it by those who honestly believe in its advisability; for those who disbelieve in it, yet enlist their powers in its behalf, no condemnation can be too strong. The first duty of the citizen is to further what he honestly believes to be the real interests of the state, and, if his activity take the special form of argument through the medium of the press, to be sure that his public utterances tally with his private opinions. To repudiate this obligation is to act the part of traitor, and in a more dangerous, because a more insidious, way than that of the leader of an armed revolt. 'To thine own self be true' is a precept that journalists, more than most other people, need to keep in mind.

Anonymity doubtless serves as a shelter for much of the baseness that we are reprobating; yet historically, Mr. Stephen tells us, it is rather the effect than the cause.

'According to a well-known anecdote, two writers of the eighteenth century decided by the toss of a halfpenny which should write for Walpole and which should write for his adversary Pulteney; but the choice was generally decided by less reputable motives. Now, so long as the press meant such a class it was of course natural that the trade should be regarded as discreditable, and should be carried on by men who had less care for their character than for their pockets. In England, where our development has been continuous and traditions linger long, the sentiment long survived; and the practice which corresponded to it — the practice, that is, of anonymity — has itself survived the sentiment which gave it birth.'

Mr. Stephen then goes on to say:

'The mask was formerly worn by men who were ashamed of their employment, and who had the same reasons for anonymity as a thief or an anarchist may have for a disguise. It may now be worn even by men who are proud of their profession, because the mask has a different significance.'

This latter statement is to a considerable extent true, but we are far from sure that the sentiment is dead that gave birth to anonymity, or that great numbers of journalists to-day do not write what they are told to write, and paid for writing, irrespective of their own convictions.

Anonymity has other dangers than the major one of making men false to themselves. It affords, for example, 'obvious conveniences to a superficial omniscience.' Mr. Stephen remarks with genial humor:

'The young gentleman who dogmatizes so early might

blush if he had to sign his name to his audacious utterances. His tone of infallibility would be absurd if we knew who was the pope that was promulgating dogmas. The man in a mask professes to detect at a glance the absurd sophistries which impose upon the keenest contemporary intellects; but if he doffed the mask and appeared as young Mr. Smith, or Jones, who took his degree last year, we might doubt whether he had a right to assume so calmly that the sophistry is all on the other side.'

The one safe rule seems to be that the anonymous writer 'should say nothing when he speaks in the plural which would make him look silly if he used the first person singular.' The man who should follow this rule, and who should refrain from allowing any personal feeling to invade his judgments of other men and their works, might safely be trusted to write unsigned articles by the score, and, if he remained all the while true to his convictions, could not fairly be charged with falling short of the whole duty of authorship.

Another temptation that besets the author is that of being content to follow current opinion, instead of doing his best to aid in its formation. 'There is an old story,' says Mr. Stephen, 'which tells how a certain newspaper used to send out an emissary to discover what was the common remark that everyone was making in omnibuses and club smoking-rooms, and to fashion it into next morning's article for the instruction of mankind. The echo affected to set the tune which it really repeated.' One of the most obvious duties of authorship is that of having something of your own to say, and of preparing yourself by strenuous effort to say it in the most direct and forcible manner. There is a great deal more of 'facile writing' than there was half a century ago, but it is doubtful if there is any more writing of the first-rate sort, 'which speaks of a full mind and strong convictions, which is clear because it is thorough.' This phase of the question of duty as it relates to authors could not be better put than in the following passage:

'I have been struck in reading newspaper articles, even my own, by the curious loss of individuality which a man seems to suffer as a writer. Unconsciously the author takes the color of his organ; he adopts not only its sentiment but its style, and seems to become a mere transmitter of messages, with whose substance he has no more to do than the wires of the electric telegraph which carries them. But now and then we suddenly come across something fresh and original; we know by instinct

TENDENCIES IN LITERATURE.

To the seasoned critic, there are few things so amusing as the habit the amateur observer has of indulging in broad generalizations concerning contemporary literature. Some book proves to be the fashion of the hour, and straightway it is made the subject of philosophizing. What is merely a ripple upon the surface of popular taste is viewed as a fresh and deep current of human thought, and this supposedly new departure of the spirit serves as a starting-point for many a solemn disquisition upon types and schools and movements. These grave inductions from a single instance, or a few instances, however philosophical the parade of the terms in which they are presented, betray their essentially unphilosophical character by the obvious inadequacy of their basis of fact. They are made only to be forgotton, as, in the majority of cases, the books that occasioned them are forgotten, after the lapse of a few years. It is not so very long ago that the American public was reading and talking 'Trilby' with such frantic enthusiasm that one would have thought a new literary era had dawned. Many were the seeming-wise reflections of which this entertaining story was the innocent provoking cause, many were the hopes, or the fears, for our literary development that took their starting point from the vogue of this particular piece of fiction. All this discussion was the work of the amateur, and we now realize how absurd it all was. The novel in question is clean forgotten to-day, and with it the whole argument based upon its success. Anyone can see now what the practiced critic saw all the time, that there was no more significance in the astonishing vogue of 'Trilby' than there had been a score of years earlier in the equally astonishing vogue of 'Helen's Babies.'

In point of fact, when the philosophical student of literature confronts the question of literary tendencies, he sees two things with absolute distinctness. One of them is that the study of tendencies, of movements, of the transformations of a nation's idealisms, is the most important thing about the history of any literature, the only in a critical rather than a creative period. As the few great survivors of the earlier age one by one pass away, we feel acutely conscious that the places are left unfilled. The season of analysis and introspection is clearly upon us. In such a period as ours, versatility, good taste, and excellent workmanship abound, and the number of good writers, as distinguished from the great masters, is astonishingly large. Sometimes they spring up in the most unexpected quarters, and anticipation flutters at the thought of a possible resurgence of the creative impulse. But we must not deceive ourselves into thinking that our bustling literary activity is swelling to any appreciable or noticeable extent the stock of the world's masterpieces. Our literature of to-day is various and entertaining, it has taste and even distinction, but it is not a literature adorned by the opulent blossoming of genius.

If we may venture, after the preceding disclaimer, to indicate any distinct tendencies in the English and American literature of the past few years, we would say that it has moved, and is still moving, in the direction of artistic freedom, of cosmopolitan interest, and of broadened social sympathy. It no longer suffers, for example, under the reproach of being produced with an exaggerated deference to the Young Person. To place under the ban whole tracts of human life, to refrain from dealing with whole groups of the most important of human relations because their treatment gives offense to immature minds, is a procedure not justified by the larger view of what literature means. This lesson we have learned of recent years. If we take into account the newest of new women and the youngest of emancipated young men, it may seem that the lesson has been too well learned, but, on the whole, out literary art has gained strength with its newly acquired freedom. Our literature is also measurably freed from its old-time provincialism of outlook. We have seen established for the mintage of the mind a broader compact than any Latin Union; if an idea have but intrinsic value, its currency does not now need to be forced in other countries than that of its origin. This, too, is a great gain, and will make the next creative period all the easier of approach. But the greatest gain of all, to our thinking, is the awakening of the new social sympathy that characterizes our recent literature. We hear a good deal of 'democratic art,' and much of what we have thus far got is distressingly crude and dull with didacticism. But the future of our race belongs to democracy, and literature must make the best of this inevitable movement. That it will eventually learn how to shape the idealism of democracy into forms of convincing beauty we make no doubt, and the signs are not wanting that such an issue is near at hand. An illustration of resounding significance may be found in the work of the greatest of living Russians. The writings of Count Tolstoy, or to be more exact, the earnest attention which they have received during the past few years, offer an impressive example of the power of the social motive, as embodied in the forms of fictive art, to make itself felt as a force in literature. Here is a writer whose whole genius is spent in an impassioned appeal to purely democratic sympathies, and, as the years go on, his figure assumes grander and grander proportions, and his utterance seems to become more and more invested with the attributes of prophecy.

ENERGY AND ART.

Mr. Swinburne speaks somewhere of the distinction, which yet amounts to 'no mutually exclusive division,' between the gods and the giants of literature. Practically the same distinction is made by his friend, Mr. Theodore Watts-Dunton, in the statement, which recurs frequently in the writings of the latter critic, to the effect that poetic energy and poetic art are 'the two forces that move in the production of all poetry.' The distinction is illuminating for the understanding of poetry, for these two forces are the fundamental elements of the effective appeal of literature, as, indeed, of all the forms of artistic endeavor. In the greatest of poets, to be sure, we find the two forces to coëxist in such supreme degree and perfect balance that they become, as it were, merely the two aspects of the phenomenon which we call genius, and we understand that for the highest achievements of literature the one is but the necessary complement of the other. This is what we find in Shakespeare and Dante and Pindar, possibly also in Goethe and Milton. But when we view the work of the poets who just escape inclusion in the small company of the supreme singers of the world, we nearly always discover some preponderance of energy over art or of art over energy. As coming under the latter category, for example, we think of Sophocles and Virgil and Tennyson; while the former category embraces Æschylus and Lucretius and Victor Hugo. Taking a step still further away from the great masters, we meet with such fairly antipodal contrasts as are offered by Horace and Juvenal, by Spenser and Jonson, or by Keats and Byron. In these cases we have either art so finished that the energy has become potential, or energy so unrestrained that the art has been well-nigh ignored.

This thought may profitably be pursued into the domain of prose literature, and even, as was above suggested, into the field of the fine arts in general. The noblest prose — that of Plato, for example — has the same balance of energy and art that is displayed by tbe noblest poetry. On the other hand, we have tremendous energy with but scant art in such a writer as Carlyle, well-nigh perfect art with but little energy in such a writer as Landor. In architecture, the Gothic style astonishes us with its energy, the classic style entrances us with its art. In sculpture, the one type is represented by Michel Angelo, the other by Thorwaldsen. In painting, the predominance of energy in Tintoretto is as unquestionable as the predominance of art in Raphael. And in music, while Bach and Beethoven stand for the Shakespearian harmony of both forces in their highest development, we may easily discern the overplus of energy in Liszt and Tschaikowsky, of art in Gluck and Mozart. The broad distinction between the classic and the romantic styles, which runs through all the arts, is, moreover, to a considerable extent, the distinction between these two primary forces under other names.

In a recent number of 'The Athenæum' there are some interesting remarks upon this subject as it is related to literary criticism, remarks in which it would be an affectation to pretend not to recognize the hand of Mr.

Watts-Dunton. 'It would be unseemly here to criticize contemporary criticism, but it may, without intending offense, be said that while the appreciation of poetry as an energy is as strong as ever in the criticism of the present day, the appreciation of poetry as an art is non-existent, except in one or two quarters which we need not indicate. . . . To go no further back than the time when Rossetti's poems were published, compare the critical canons then in vogue with the critical canons of the present day. On account of a single cockney rhyme, the critics of that period would damn a set of verses in which perhaps a measure of poetic energy was not wanting. The critics of to-day fall for the most part into two classes: those who do not know what is meant by a cockney rhyme, and those who love a cockney rhyme.' If this is true, it is a serious matter, for we are not content to share the non-committal position of the writer, who confines himself to saying: 'We merely record an interesting and suggestive fact of literary history. If in poetical criticism the wisdom of one generation is the folly of the next, it is the same in everything man says and in everything he does, so whimsical a creature has the arch-humorist Nature set at the top of the animal kingdom.'

For our part, we believe that the appreciation of poetry as an art is essential to the very existence of criticism, and are far from willing to admit that it is non-existent at the present day. It is true enough that a great deal of verbiage about poetry issues from the 'blind mouths' of self-constituted critics who know not whereof they speak; but that has always been the case. Our writer himself makes the saving admission that the art of poetry still finds appreciation 'in one or two quarters which we need not indicate,' and that is probably all that might be said of the criticism of Rossetti's time, or of a still earlier generation. When we are well along into the twentieth century, it is precisely the criticism from these unindicated quarters that will alone survive, and will urge the writers of that period in turn to say things about the decay of criticism in their own time. The ineptitudes of the criticism that greeted the early work of Keats and Shelley, of Wordsworth and Tennyson, were surely as unfortunate as any utterances of the present day, and, what is particularly to the point, they were lacking in precisely that appreciation of poetry as art for which Mr. Watts-Dunton seeks almost in vain in our current critical literature.

Having entered this protest against a statement that seems altogether too sweeping, we are now prepared to admit that a good many present-day facts lend countenance to the contention. Popular opinion naturally cares more for energy than for art in literature, for the obvious reason that it is stirred by the one and not easily susceptible to the appeal of the other. It feels the power of Browning, for example, and, although by long familiarity made dimly conscious of the exquisite art of Tennyson, is disposed to allow the one quality to offset the other, and consider the two as equally great poets. It is the same rough-and-ready sort of judgment that for a long time held Byron to be a greater poet than Wordsworth, that in our own time thinks of Tolstoi as a greater master of fiction than Tourguénieff, or that made Juvenal seem a greater poet than Virgil to the individual idiosyncrasy of Hugo, or Wordsworth and even